EX LIBRIS

Jordan Lee Harding

TORONTO, MY CITY

A Photographic Memoir
BY

KIM ONDAATJE

Quarry Press

The publisher gratefully acknowledges the
assistance of the Canada Council, the Ontario
Arts Council, the Department of
Communications, and the Ontario Publishing
Centre.

Canadian Cataloguing in Publication Data

Ondaatje, Kim 1928-
Toronto, my city : a photographic memoir

ISBN 1-55082-062-1

1. Toronto (Ont.) — Pictorial works, I. Title

FC3097.37.063 1993 971.3'541'00222
F1059.5.T684063 1993 C93-090071-5

Design by Keith Abraham.
Typeset by Quarry Press Inc.
Printed and bound in Canada by Best-Gagné
Book Manufacturers, Toronto, Ontario.

Published by
Quarry Press, Inc.,
P.O. Box 1061, Kingston, Ontario K7L 4Y5.

INTRODUCTION

The seed for *Toronto, My City* was planted in Malcolm Lester's office about ten years ago. I had dropped in at Lester, Orpen & Dennys on Sullivan Street to discuss the reprinting of *Small Churches of Canada*. To the left of the entrance was the high ceilinged, once-upon-a-time livingroom painted an off-white with book cases lining the walls. An attractive young woman sat behind the desk in front of the large south window. She told me to go upstairs to Malcolm's office. I found him at his desk behind a small mountain of books about Toronto: it was around the time of the sesquicentennial celebrations. He looked up, and noticing that I was reading the titles, commented, "It would be interesting to see Toronto through the eyes of an artist. I would like to publish such a book, but not at this time when the market is flooded with books about the city."

I have a knack for undertaking projects that can never be finished. The subject is always changing, growing, disappearing, or hiding somewhere waiting to be discovered. I told Malcolm that I would love to do such a book, but that it would take me years. "That's fine. Take your time," and I did. It took so long that by the time I had taken hundreds — more truthfully thousands — of photographs of Toronto, edited them, had the survivors enlarged and then arranged them in sections, the publishing house on Sullivan Street was in financial difficulties. Within a year the shelves that held so many beautiful books were empty, and Lester, Orpen & Dennys no longer existed.

My fat manuscript of photographs sandwiched between two black leather covers sat on a side table here at Blueroof Farm, the century home bed and breakfast I own north of Kingston near Bellrock, Ontario. It was disturbed only by the occasional guest interested in photography until one day when Barbara Allen and Wayne Oakley of Kingston's Printed Passage bookstore came for lunch. After lunch while Barb and I were talking, Wayne looked through the photographs. As he was leaving he asked if he could show them to a friend who was also interested in photography. The friend was Bob Hilderley, and that is how — by a stroke of serendipity — the fat, black manuscript found a publisher and its way to Quarry Press in Kingston.

As an artist, I feel that anything on a page or a canvas other than the intended composition is a distraction and that a title tends to limit a viewer's experience of the work. The ideal book, in my opinion, would be the fat, black manuscript itself. The cost of reproducing all these eight by ten photographs would be prohibitive, especially in these difficult times. I tell my students to shoot only when the feeling is strong. Each picture I take means something special to me, and those not included are as important as those that are. Final selection decisions have to be objective; the task fell on my publisher and the book's designer Keith Abraham. They had to decide what might be of most interest to others.

Why have I called the collection "My City"? Partly because I was born in Toronto at what was then 1400 Avenue Road, an estate at the very north end of the city on property now known as Kimbark Boulevard. My earliest memory is of the paving of Avenue Road above Glencairne Avenue. In the thirty-five years I have lived in Toronto and the thirty I have experienced it as a visitor, I have watched it grow from a city about the size of present day London, Ontario into a vast, exciting, and sophisticated metropolis. I lived in Toronto in the seventies, when David Crombie was mayor, and served on his advisory committee on design which was involved in the struggle for the preservation and restoration of downtown neighbourhoods, the careful development of the waterfront, the creation of trails for cyclists and hikers, and a host of other things. After a couple of years of sitting through committee meetings, I was set free with my camera to create a slide documentary to support a presentation to City Council by illustrating the role a downtown neighbourhood can play in preventing an area from becoming a shabby, litter strewn jungle of concrete and dust.

By the time the project was finished, I realized a little of how much a building and its details can tell about past and present day owners, and I began to branch out and explore the city area by area. Often I was lost and had no idea where I was when I took a shot. All I knew was the general district I was exploring that particular day. If someone should set out to find a particular place that I have photographed, they may or may not find it, but I can guarantee that they will find other places of interest. Toronto is rich territory for the artist or tourist who likes to explore.

8

Finally, I want to thank Bob Hilderley for doing a job I could not do, and Henry Yee who can print not only what is on the film, but what my intentions were in shooting it. I also want to warn any purchaser of this book that I am not an architect or a historian. My life on this farm allows little time for writing and none for research, and since any information I might give is likely to be incorrect, I have written as little as possible. *Toronto, My City* is just part of a personal record of what I saw and felt and loved and nothing else.

Kim Ondaatje
Blueroof Farm, Bellrock, Ontario

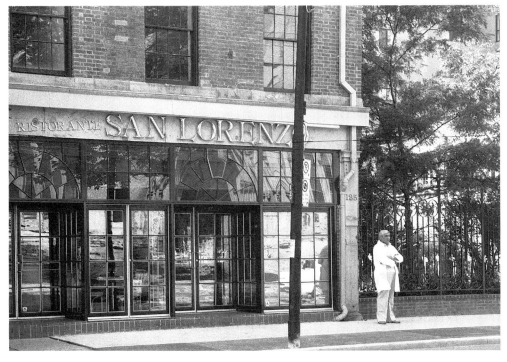

REFLECTIONS

From the shining waters of Lake Ontario to the glass walls of downtown skyscrapers, from the still ponds of formal gardens to the polished windows of quiet neighborhoods, Toronto is a city of reflections. Contemporary architects have designed structures like Ontario Place and the Ontario Hydro Building at the corner of College Street and University Avenue to bring a special light to bear upon the city. I remember attending the free concerts at Ontario Place during the summer where the joy of listening to the music under the stars was heightened by watching the sparkling reflections on the black and sometimes moving mirror of the lake. Glass buildings like the Ontario Hydro Building mirror the sky almost perfectly during the day — perhaps too perfectly as I have read that flocks of birds have flown into it with the result that different colours of glass have subsequently been used on such towers to alert birds of danger — and during December evenings these glass palaces multiply the Christmas lights, turning the downtown area, especially lower University Avenue, into a veritable fantasy land.

While architects have enhanced this mirror effect by placing reflecting pools around the buildings, landscape gardeners have designed public gardens centered around ponds and lagoons which reflect so beautifully what is floating on them or standing beside them. In winter these transparent mirrors often become skating rinks like those at City Hall or Ryerson, where a large boulder at centre ice gives the skater a sense of the wilderness in the midst of the city while circling the rink. Even interior and commercial designers seem to be captivated by this spirit, creating fountains and foyers, like those at Roy Thomson Hall and the Toronto Stock Exchange, which seem to reflect the artistic and commercial life of Toronto, however darkly or clearly.

As an artist — a painter and photographer — I am especially intrigued by hues of light. Viewed from Centre Island during the day, the Toronto skyline looks like an abstract sculpture hewn out of rock, concrete, and black glass with a hunk of dazzling gold in the middle. This view changes completely in the evening. I remember sitting on the edge of the front lawn of the Royal Canadian Yacht Club watching the sun set behind the city. As twilight deepened, the hard city grew softer and softer, less abstract, until the stark image became fragile with window lights glowing through the darkness. The solid city turned before my eyes into a fairyland of matchsticks and light — something you could topple over with the brush of a hand.

Still, there is something stubborn in me that makes me admire Toronto's old stone and wooden buildings, especially the churches and houses that survive and thrive while the world of commerce impinges upon them. Many of the old houses were built by members of the city's first families or they were the original farmhouse in

the area. It's fun to walk around a residential neighbourhood and try to spot the original farmhouse or elegant country home. The old churches are easier to find as they stand out on main streets or at key intersections like the little Methodist Church on the north side of Finch Avenue West or the church — almost at the centre of the city — standing staunchly on the northeast corner of Avenue Road and Bloor Street West. These churches underscore the contrasts in architectural styles which reflect the changing tastes of generations of Torontonians. The world of commerce and the world of spirit are not always at odds, though. One spring day I was walking along the south side of Bloor Street east of Yonge Street when I suddenly caught a glimpse of a new church with a glass steeple and bell tower in perfect harmony with the glistening business towers surrounding it.

← Down to Merchants Mall   Restaurants Subway

18-29

SPECIAL PLACES

After the Second World War, Toronto changed incredibly in character. Gradually dozens of small galleries and theatres sprang up, especially downtown, and hundreds, perhaps thousands, of intimate and ethnic restaurants enriched not only the central core of the city but also various neighbourhoods. Some of these places hold a lasting place in my heart, even though some have disappeared. My favourite little restaurant is Le Select Bistro on Queen Street West. The wide sidewalk leading to the door reminds me of the little cafés in Paris I visited while a student; inside, the walls are lined with theatre posters. The tables at Le Select Bistro are so tiny that some ingenious person got the idea of hanging the bread basket above them on a rope running through a ceiling ring and secured by a cleat conveniently placed near the table. The sailor in me enjoys lowering the bread like a sail.

Other Toronto places have always intrigued and rewarded me, especially the residential areas of the Annex, Cabbagetown, Chinatown, Rosedale, the Beaches, Forest Hill, and the neighbourhoods west of Spadina. As I walk through these neighbourhoods, the houses that most interest me have porches, extending the mystery of their interior life out to the passerby on the sidewalk. There is something inviting and gracious and intimate about a porch or verandah, something that reminds me of the wonderful summer homes and cottages I have known, a memory especially welcome in the midst of a hot July day in the city. In Forest Hill and Rosedale I especially enjoy the blooming shrubs and distinctive flowerbeds that adorn the wide lots and give character to houses that otherwise share a certain sameness of good taste.

In the Annex, Cabbagetown, Kensington Market, or parts of the West End where the houses are closely knit, there is something different every twenty-five feet or so that gives me a clue, kindles my imagination, or arouses my curiosity about the people who live in these colourful houses with their low-fenced yards. Sometimes grapes hang heavy from trellises, tomato plants thrive in yards the size of quilts, unexpected pieces of kitsch or natural pieces of found art suddenly appear behind all kinds of hedges and borders. The sense of private ownership and neighbourhood pride is overwhelming. These tiny yards reflect something of the owner's creativity, ethnic background, ingenuity, religious belief, practical bent, or just plain laziness that is always interesting and often refreshing. Walks through these neighbourhoods are never dull, especially if you wander along side alleys to discover backyards just as interesting.

The downtown core of the city is also full of little surprises — tiny parks, sudden courtyards, water trickling down a wall, a yard full of statues of cows — but what most intrigues me is the way people use these spaces, especially at lunch time as they seek respite from work to eat or read alone. In my own life, I have been aware of how alone a person can feel in the midst of a city populated by hundreds of thousands, and with my camera I have never had difficulty finding subjects who reflect that unsettling experience.

Art

Like the surprising folk art found in some neighbourhoods, the pedestrian in Toronto happens across some wonderful works of fine art outside of the city's many public and private galleries. In vacant lots, at the St. Lawrence Market, on the backside of the "Flat Iron" building on Front Street, in the handmade wooden storekeeper signs, in the graffiti and wall murals, I have found much that captures my attention. Especially fascinating are the little sculpture parks scattered around the city. One of the oldest in the city is located at the corner of St. Clair Avenue and Avenue Road where the replica of the Peter Pan statue from London's Hyde Park stands under tall shade trees. Another favourite park is located at the corner of St. Clair Avenue and Mount Pleasant Road where a memorial has been erected in honour of the famous women sculptors Frances Loring and Florence Wyle who lived and worked in an old church studio on nearby Glenrose Avenue. Yet another memorial stands serenely in High Park, a tribute to the European woman poet Lesya Ukrainka (1871–1913), erected in 1975 by the Women's Council of the Ukranian Canadian Committee. These small art treasures are not dwarfed in spirit by the large downtown Henry Moore sculptures outside the Art Gallery of Ontario and the new City Hall, or the Michael Snow works integrated into that monument to sports and entertainment, the SkyDome.

GARDENS

When you fly over Toronto during the summer in a small plane, the many treed ravines, parks, cemeteries, and gardens make the city look like a forest. The Scarborough Bluffs and Toronto Island as well as High Park, Edward's Gardens, and James Garden create wonderful settings for family picnics and weddings. Allan Gardens, with a vast array of flora under glass, brings a taste of summer to the coldest winter day. Although somewhat more reverend and funereal, cemeteries like Mount Pleasant offer the greatest possible variety of trees and shrubs with a full display of leaves and blooms. Like the small sculpture gardens, I most appreciate the unexpected gardens and parks found at the end of a cul de sac, at the foot of some towering building, at the entrance to a ravine, or in a vacant

lot. The more challenging and difficult the times become, the greater the need for these tiny places. Without them, Toronto would become just another cold, northern city, not a refreshing "city of gardens." Trees make such a difference! I remember my husband complaining years ago when we lived in the "new" neighbourhood of Don Mills that he could not tell which house was ours since they all looked alike. I planted twenty-one trees on the front lawn so that he could find his way home.

Toronto, the apparently staid and conservative capital of Ontario, is not without a spirit of play. Riverdale Farm, located on the site of the old Toronto Zoo in the Don Valley ravine, is an unexpected source of pleasure, where you can hear a rooster crow above the sounds of city traffic and watch children patting the ponies and learning about

ЛЕСЯ

the character of animals. Perhaps one of the best places to visit if you wish to have some fun is Ontario Place, especially the colourful punching bag forest, with children darting between the swaying, elongated blue, red, and yellow bags. Or you can find yourself spell-bound playing a variation of the "Where's Waldo" kind of game while watching people cross the bridge from the mainland to the park. Reflections on the underlying water only double the fun. The Ontario Science Centre, with its vine-covered concrete walls blending into the Don Valley landscape, offers a rare blend of education and entertainment — and a rare opportunity for colour landscape photography, especially in the early spring and fall when it almost disappears into the sides of the ravine. If Ontario Place or the Ontario Science Centre seem too contemporary or high tech for your taste, the city offers the historically-minded such heritage sites as Old Fort York and Black Creek Pioneer Village.

ENVOI

If the best things in life are free, people who live in Toronto are fortunate. There is much for them and their guests to see, to explore, and to remember without spending any — or very little — money. This city of great natural, architectural, artistic, and spiritual treasures does not demand riches to enjoy. As I wandered about the city taking these pictures and reflecting upon my feelings for Toronto, my pockets were full of film, filters, or lens caps, but never money. Now that I live in Southeastern Ontario on a farm near Bellrock, I've come to believe that my old home, Toronto, has the potential to become the finest city of the twenty-first century. The peculiarly urban problems that have to be solved may seem staggering, but as long as Torontonians find a way of working together and working hard, they can live in the finest city in the world.

LIST OF PLATES